is your name
DAVI(E)S

nicholas gould

Published by Kenneth Mason
The old harbourmaster's, Emsworth, Hants
© Nicholas Gould 1983

British Library Cataloguing in
Publication Data

Gould, Nicholas
    Is your name Davies.
    1. Davies (Name)
    I. Title
    929'.2'0942   CS2508.D/

ISBN 0-85937-310-X

Typeset and produced by Articulate Studios,
Emsworth, Hampshire.
Printed by Conifer Press, Gosport, Hampshire

THE ORIGIN OF THE NAME DAVIES

DAVIES IS THE SIXTH commonest English surname. (If the total for the alternative spelling Davis is added, the combination narrowly beats Williams into third place, after Smith and Jones.) Many people would object to my first sentence, on the grounds that Davies is not an English surname, but a Welsh one. This is quite true, of course: nowadays, the spelling Davies is most commonly found in people of Welsh descent, while Davis is the normal English form. But both are in origin the same name, which is my excuse for dealing with them together. And the meaning and history of both names can best be understood in the context of English surnames in general. (I hope I shall not ruffle the feelings of too many Davises if for the rest of this discussion I use the spelling Davies to stand for both.)

Every English surname falls into one of four categories. There are Surnames of Relationship (where the original holder was identified as a relation — usually a son — of someone else) like Rogerson, Rogers, Hodge, Hodgkin, Dodgson: Surnames of Location (describing where the original holder lived or came from) like Bridge, Dale, Waters, North, Easton, Lincoln, Scott: Surnames from Nicknames, like Brown, Whitehead, Young, Armstrong, Lord and Lamb: and Surnames of Occupation (describing what the original holder did) like Archer, Goldsmith, Tyler, Brewer, Cartwright or Glover. All these types of name were originally used as straight descriptions of individuals: a man called Richard who was the son of a well-known local figure called David might be known as Richard Davidson to distinguish him from the other people in the village also called Richard — perhaps one of them might be called Richard Hill (because he lived on the hill), another Richard Gray (because he had grey hair), and a third Richard Smith (because he was the village blacksmith). In the course of the Middle Ages these second names gradually became hereditary, passed down from father to son. In about 1100, if Richard Davidson himself had a son called John, he would have been called John Richardson (or some other appropriate description). In 1400 he might very likely have been called John Davidson despite the fact that he was not himself David's son; for by then Davidson had become a true surname in the modern sense.

This account simplifies things a good deal. Most importantly, I may have implied that if a man took his second name from the fact that his father was called David, that second name would inevitably have taken the form Davidson. There are in fact many other surnames which originally meant 'David's son', and one of them is of course Davies. The christian name plain and simple might be used: David is still found as a surname today. An ending -s might be added, giving the sense 'of David', with 'son' understood. And each of these three basic types, with -son, with -s, and with no added ending, could be used with any of a great variety of forms of the original christian name. A mediaeval David might be better known by some pet-form of his name, such as Daw, Day, Davy, Dawkin or Dow. All these and other variants are the source of modern surnames. So Davies, first recorded in Cambridgeshire in 1327 (actually in the spelling Davisse), is just one of a family of names of identical meaning, such as Davidson, Davison, Davy, Daw, Dawes, Dawson, Dawkins, Day, Dow and Dowson.

If, then, you were born with the surname Davis, it is likely that you are directly descended from someone whose christian name was David, and whose son's second name Davies, meaning 'David's son', was passed on to his descendants. I say likely, for nothing in surname study is 100% certain. Davies, and similar names with that -s ending, were used to describe not merely a man's children, but his dependants of other sorts: so 'servant of David', for example, may be the correct interpretation in a few cases. The vast majority of Davieses, however, are certainly descended from men called David. Some of these men (and probably most of those whose descendants spell their name Davis) were English, but far more were Welsh

Welsh surnames

TRUE HEREDITARY SURNAMES of the English type developed late in Wales. The traditional Welsh way of labelling a man was to use the word *ap* or *ab* meaning 'son of', followed by the father's name — Morgan ap Richard, Hugh ap Rhys, William ab Evan. (A vestige of this ap or ab survives in such modern surnames as Pritchard, Price and Bevan.) The Welsh have always been fascinated by genealogy, and consequently often went further than this, listing a man's pedigree for several generations back, such as John ap Robert ap Griffith ap Madoc. This habit was one the English found vastly amusing and made the subject of many jokes and tall stories. A comic poet described Cheese as 'Ap Curds, ap Milk, ap Cow, ap Grass, ap Earth.' One of the longer anecdotes concerned an Englishman riding one dark night among the Welsh mountains, who heard a cry for help from a deep ravine by the roadside. 'Who's there?' he asked. 'Jenkin ap Griffith ap Robin ap William ap Rees ap Evan', came the reply. 'Lazy fellows that you be', retorted the Englishman, setting spurs to his horse, 'to lie rolling in that hole, half a dozen of ye; why, in the name of common sense, don't ye help one another out?'

It was only in the 16th century that what the English thought of as 'normal' surnames began to catch on in Wales. The Tudors were a Welsh family, and from Henry VII's reign onwards increasing numbers of Welshmen began to emigrate to England to seek their fortunes. There, it was natural for them to adopt English surnames; and the obvious surnames to adopt were the anglicized versions of their native ones. So an Ap William (or strictly speaking Ap Gwilym) would become known as Williams, an Ap David (Ap Dafydd) as Davies, an Ap John (Ap Ioan) as Jones, and so on. The process was not confined to Welsh immigrants to England. Back home, too, the pressure was on for Welshmen to become more English. One political development hastened the change. In 1536 Henry VIII's government passed the Act of Union of England and Wales: its intention, which happily did not succeed, was to achieve complete uniformity — to eliminate the Welshness of Wales. A proper hereditary surname was one of the signs that a Welshman had become anglicized.

The Welsh gentry, seeing which way the wind was blowing, adapted fairly rapidly, and did their best to turn into facsimile Englishmen. Among the common people change came much more slowly, to the despair of generations of English bureaucrats. As late as 1853 the Registrar General could complain, 'Among the lower classes in the wilder districts . . . the christian name of the father still frequently becomes the patronymic of the son.' In 1891 a case heard in a London court involved a man from Caernarvonshire who was uncertain of his own surname. His christian name was Henry and his father was Thomas Evans, but he referred to himself indifferently as Henry Evans, Henry Thomas, and Henry Thomas Evans!

Even when the majority of Welsh people had finally adopted hereditary surnames, another problem remained. For centuries the Welsh had extensively used only a small number of christian names: and when they adopted surnames they made far less use than mediaeval Englishmen of

Uncle Davis . . . the pawnbroker

occupational names, nicknames and local names. Moreover most of their patronymic surnames took only one or two possible forms from each christian name: there was no Welsh equivalent of the English proliferation of Davidsons and Dawsons and Dawkinses and Dawses. In consequence modern Wales is cursed with a very limited choice of overwhelmingly common surnames, to an extent which has become a standing joke. (Eg Englishman in Wales, seeing factory sign, *Jones Manufacturing Company*, mutters, 'So that's where they make them.') In the 19th century there was a serious proposal that a change-of-name registry should be set up in Wales to encourage greater diversity.

No such step was ever taken, and the problem remains. Surnames arose to distinguish one man from another: Welsh surnames have manifestly failed in this, their primary function, and consequently many people have added a further distinguishing label. This can be a formal one, the hyphenated name (often originally formed by combining the names of mother and father), such as Williams-Ellis, Lloyd-Davies or Bowen-Jones. The revival of early Welsh christian names like Geraint, Idris, Gareth and Emrys has added some variety and distinctiveness (it is noteworthy that such names, with a few exceptions, seldom occur as surnames — they were not in use during the crucial period from the 16th to the 19th century). Then again, many distinguished Welshmen, poets in particular, have for the last two centuries or so been better known by pseudonyms taken from place-names or early Welsh history and literature. But most common of all are the unofficial nicknames familiar from accounts of Welsh village life. A man may be named from his trade or workplace, his home or place of origin, some personal characteristic or even some chance phrase which, once used, is never forgotten by the community — an exact parallel, in fact, to the way in which surnames originated in England. Some such additional names may even become hereditary, suggesting that the whole process of surname formation is being started again from scratch.

How many Davieses are there, where?

NOBODY KNOWS how many Davieses there are in the world, but it is possible to give an approximate figure on the basis of some estimates which have been made. In Britain as a whole, Davies comes sixth after Smith, Jones, Williams, Brown and Taylor: but if the score for Davis is added, the combined names move up into third place. A count was recently made of all the entries in the birth, marriage and death registers for England and Wales for the first quarter of 1975. This gave a total of nearly 395,000 entries, a large enough sample to be representative, and of these 2,753 had the surname Davies, and 941 Davis. (For comparison, Smith scored 6,723, Jones 5,521, and Williams 3,621.) This suggests that about one person in 143 in England and Wales is a Davies and one in 419 a Davis — perhaps 340,000 and 117,000 people respectively. In the USA, oddly enough, the position of the two variant spellings is reversed, and Davis is far commoner than Davies — an estimated 1,100,000 as against only 40,000. If we add to these totals the probable number in Canada, Australia, New Zealand and other communities of British descent, we arrive at a world total of around 500,000 for Davies and 1,250,000 for Davis.

Obviously, the two surnames are not evenly distributed throughout Britain. Evidence for this is patchy, and more research is badly needed. The only detailed survey of this aspect of surname study was made in 1890 by H B Guppy in his book *The Homes of Family Names.* Guppy analysed the distribution of surnames among English and Welsh farmers, as being 'the most stay-at-home class of the country.' Surname scholars are still arguing about Guppy's findings and disputing whether his samples were as representative as he claimed: but they are of interest in the absence of anything better. He confirms the general belief that Davies is the Welsh spelling and Davis the English one. In Wales Guppy found between five and six per cent of farmers surnamed Davies. In Herefordshire Davies scored 2.5 per cent and in Shropshire only slightly less: in each county Davis was one-fifth as common or less. The only other English counties where Davies outnumbered Davis were Cheshire, Lancashire and Cornwall. In most of the eastern and northern counties Guppy found neither form of the name common enough to be worth counting. He points out that on the east coast

Farmer Davis

its place is largely taken by Davey or Davy, and in the North and Scotland by Davidson or Davison.

The simplest way to test Guppy's figures would be to compare them with those from the modern telephone directories; telephone owners are probably sufficiently numerous today to be a representative sample of the population as a whole. A systematic survey would be enormously time-consuming, but I have done a few rough counts. These suggest that nearly a century of population movement has lessened the numerical differences between areas, and in particular that Davies has gained ground relative to Davis over most of England. But much of Guppy's general distribution pattern is still valid. The percentage of Welsh Davieses ranges from about 2.5 per cent in northern and central Wales to more than three per cent in Cardiff and the south-east. In Swansea and the south-west Davies is the commonest name, with more than six per cent, outnumbering even Jones: would it be far-fetched to see this as a result of the popularity of Saint David in that area, leading to a greater number of children christened David over the centuries, and hence a greater number of Davieses?

Outside Wales, I can detect no clear pattern in the relative frequency of Davies and Davis. Of the directories studied (30 or so), Davis outnumbered Davies only in six (London, Glasgow, Gloucester area, Bath and west Wiltshire, and both parts of Ireland); but over much of England Davis ran Davies fairly close, neither name being exceptionally common. Guppy's remarks about alternative names in the north and east seem to be borne out. In the Norwich area the combined score for Davey, Davy and Davie is 252, beating Davis with 191, and not too far short of Davies with 324. In Newcastle both Davison with 673 and Davidson with 420 outnumber Davies and Davis with 325 each, and the figures for Scotland are more striking still — in Aberdeen and the north-east there are about 1,340 Davidsons, whereas Davies and Davis, with 88 and 32, hardly get a look in. All these figures go to show that despite the population shifts of modern times the average person in Britain still lives in more or less the same region of the country as his ancestors did.

Nicknames for Davieses

SOME SURNAMES have what are known as 'inseparable' nicknames connected with them — nicknames which can be given to a man simply on the strength of his surname, without reference to anything else about him. 'Chalky' White, 'Dusty' Miller, and 'Nobby' Clark are three well-known examples. Such names were most often found in the Army and Navy; I am not sure how many of them are still in everyday use. The inseparable nickname for a Davies or Davis, whether Welsh or English, is Taffy. This of course is a Welsh form of Davy or David. (As David has long been one of the most popular christian names in Wales, Taffy is also used when addressing a Welshman whose name one does not know. In the same way an unfamiliar Irishman may be addressed as Paddy or Mick, a Scot as Jock or Sandy, and an Englishman as John.)

M'Lud Davies . . . the judge

' *Running after women never hurt anybody — it's catching 'em that does the damage* ' **Jack Davies,** English writer

SOME FAMOUS — AND INFAMOUS — DAVIESES

The tramp poet: William Henry Davies (1871-1940)

'WHEN I WAS between 13 and 14 I wanted to be a man of great literary genius; but when I was between 17 and 18 my ambition was to rob the rich by force and kill Indians for sport.' So wrote W H Davies in *A Poet's Pilgrimage*. As things turned out, it was the earlier of these two ambitions that was achieved, though nobody could have foreseen it at the time. Davies in his teens was not the sort of boy for whom one would have predicted a brilliant future. Expelled from school for leading a gang of shoplifters, reluctantly apprenticed to a picture-framer and spending his earnings on drink, he must have been the despair of the grandparents who brought him up in Newport in Monmouthshire. (Most people, incidentally, assume that Davies was Welsh; in fact, although his mother's roots were in Wales, his father was a Cornishman.)

When Davies was 21 his grandmother died and he came into an inheritance — not a lump sum, but an income of ten shillings a week. Even in those days this was no fortune: it was, however, enough to insure against actual starvation, and enabled Davies, now leading a drifting life in London and Bristol, to make a fresh start. He persuaded his grandmother's trustee to advance him £15, and in June 1893 sailed for New York. Thereafter for nearly six years he tramped the United States. His experiences are memorably recounted in *The Autobiography of a Super-Tramp*. Sometimes he would find casual work for a while; several times he went across the Atlantic and back on cattle boats; one winter he and a fellow hobo found a succession of warm lodgings in Michigan jails. Often he lived, and lived well, by begging: years later he was to maintain that being a famous poet in England paid less well than being a beggar in America! He learned the dangerous art of 'riding the rods' — travelling for nothing by jumping on and off moving freight trains. And it was while so engaged, in March 1899, that he had an accident which cost him his right leg.

Crippled, Davies returned to England and for the next seven years lived in a succession of common lodging houses. Yet paradoxically the accident, which had left him incapable of hard physical activity, revived his old ambition to be a writer. He produced poems, plays and essays which no publisher would consider. Once, in desperation, he starved for a fortnight to pay for 2000 copies of a single sheet of his best poems to be printed: these he hawked from door to door in the London suburbs. At the end of a wasted day, realising that he had hopelessly overestimated the public demand for poetry, he returned in disgust to his lodging and burned all 2000, 'taking care not to save one copy that would at any time in the future remind me of my folly.'

Most men would have given up at this point, but not Davies. Some time later, after heroic sacrifices, he was able to pay £19 to have a book of poems, *The Soul's Destroyer*, printed. He sent copies to well-known reviewers and men of letters, including Bernard Shaw and Edward Thomas. Articles praising his poems began to appear, and suddenly he found himself famous. The idea of a one-legged tramp in a London doss-house turning out to be a great poet caught the public imagination. A friend rented a cottage for him, and though he never became a rich man, at least his serious financial worries were over. For the rest of his life he was able to devote himself to his writing, and to the company of many friends he made in literary and artistic circles.

Davies regarded himself primarily as a poet. His prose works were to him mere pot-boilers; even *The Autobiography of a Super-Tramp* was of value to him chiefly because, as he said many years later, it had brought him in a steady 15 shillings a week since its publication in 1908. Yet most people would now regard it as his masterpiece — a plain, unselfconscious account of his extraordinary life on the road in America and his struggles to launch himself as a writer in England. As for his poems, it is fair to say that he wrote too many, too much alike. Some of his best poems draw upon his own experience of mankind: tramps, labourers, prostitutes, children, sailors are depicted with sympathy for the misery and squalor of their lives and recognition of the contrasting humanity which still shines through.

His other main theme is nature and the English countryside. He did not see these things with the eye of a naturalist or a born countryman; he admits in one poem, 'I. . . cannot know the barley from the oats, Nor call the bird by note, nor name a star.' Take birds, for example: in all his poetry only a few are mentioned specifically, and those the ones hardly anyone could mistake — robin, cuckoo, wren, lark, sparrow, kingfisher, nightingale. Even such simple distinctions as that between crows and rooks seem to have eluded him. He sees nature through the eyes of a child, observing everything, but understanding and interpreting nothing. And at its best this is his strength. Most of us are so anxious to *know* that we forget to *see*. We can learn from Davies: and has the lesson ever been expressed more simply and charmingly than in these lines from *Leisure*?

What is this life if, full of care,
We have no time to stand and stare?
No time to stand beneath the boughs
And stare as long as sheep or cows.
No time to see, as woods we pass,
Where squirrels hide their nuts in grass . . .
A poor life this if, full of care,
We have no time to stand and stare.

The father of Arctic exploration: John Davis (1550?-1605)

JOHN DAVIS, like so many of the great Elizabethan seamen, was a Devon man: he may have been a boyhood friend of Walter Raleigh. We know nothing of his early life at sea, but in 1585-7 he was put in command of three expeditions to look for the Northwest Passage. From about 1550 to 1615 the English were obsessed with the idea of finding a northern sea route to China, to break the Spanish stranglehold on eastern trade. At first the Northeast Passage, round the top of Russia, was tried: but in 1576 Humphrey Gilbert, another famous sailor and a friend of Davis, argued that a shorter and better route might be found round the north of America, a suggestion which eventually led to Davis's expeditions.

On his first voyage, in 1585, Davis and his men rounded the southern tip of Greenland and sailed north-west to the region around modern Godthaab. Here they landed and met their first Eskimos. There were four musicians on the expedition, and they played while the other Englishmen danced. This novel approach won over the Eskimos, and there was some trading done. Davis's men bought five kayaks and a great many Eskimo clothes, so much better suited than their own to the Arctic climate. Then they sailed across the strait still named after Davis, and explored part of Baffin Island. David named some prominent landmarks after his friends and sponsors back home — Mount Raleigh, Cape Walsingham, Cape Dyer, Cumberland Sound. This last is a wide channel cutting half-way through Baffin Island, and as he sailed up it Davis understandably began to think he had found the Northwest Passage. Winter was approaching, and he did not go far enough to discover his mistake. But he returned to England in high hopes.

With this optimistic report it was easy for Davis to find backers for another voyage the next year. Once again, the English landed first in Greenland, to revisit their Eskimo friends of the year before. Davis was unusual for his time in his determination to treat the natives well: his tolerance was tested later, for the Eskimos proved 'marvellous thievish, especially for iron.' In the end Davis fired two cannon to scare them off, but would not shoot at them, even when they peppered his ships with slingstones and his men urged him to retaliate. They had just arranged a truce when the wind changed and Davis set out for Baffin Island again. He sailed south down the coast, missed the entrance to Hudson Strait (which spared him the disappointment of entering Hudson Bay, immensely promising but another dead end), and reached Labrador. Here they made a marvellous catch of cod, which they salted and brought home. It must have paid some of the costs of the expedition, but it was a poor substitute for the silks and spices of China.

Nevertheless Davis, who was evidently a persuasive talker, managed to get financial backing for one more voyage. This time he sailed north up the west coast of Greenland for 1000 miles, and was driven back by the pack-ice and fog of Baffin Bay. He made no more northern voyages: even his optimism ('the passage is most probable, the execution easy', he wrote on his return) was not sufficient to coax more money from the canny merchants of Devon and London. So Davis did not find the Northwest Passage: but neither did anyone else, until Amundsen in 1905. It turned out to be much longer and more difficult than anyone in the 16th century had imagined, and not really possible with the ships they had then. But although Davis failed in his chief objective, he ranks as one of the greatest English explorers of that age. He was a brilliant navigator, and his readings of latitude during his voyages were unusually accurate. He wrote several books which became standard works on seamanship, and invented navigating instruments which were still in use two centuries later.

The rest of his story must be told more briefly. In 1591 he joined Sir Thomas Cavendish in what proved a disastrous attempt to sail round the world. (Davis was hoping for another go at the Passage, this time from the Pacific end.) The ships were separated in the Magellan Strait by 'an outrageous storm in a hell-dark night.' Only by superb courage and skill did Davis get back home, with 15 men left alive out of a crew of 76, after surviving for months on a diet of dried penguins. After this he went on several voyages to the East Indies, until in 1605 off Malaya some Japanese pirates, whom he had found in a disabled junk and tried to help, treacherously attacked and killed him.

Debtor Davis . . . the borrower

Bette Davis

WHEN BETTE DAVIS first arrived in Hollywood, so the story goes, the man sent from the studio to meet her missed her at the station, and later gave as his excuse, 'No one faintly like an actress got off the train.' One sees his point: certainly no other major star had so little going for her in the matter of looks. She herself confessed, 'When I saw my first film test I ran from the projection room screaming' — it came as a surprise to her to see how lop-sided her mouth was when she spoke.

Looks, clearly, aren't everything, even in Hollywood, for Bette Davis went on to become a screen immortal, one of the most indestructible stars the cinema ever produced. Her unique style with its clipped speech and flamboyant gestures took her straight to the top and kept her there for more than 30 years. Partly this was a result of sheer determination to succeed. 'If Hollywood didn't work out,' she says, 'I was all prepared to be the best secretary in the world.' Success on the screen did not come by being sweet and gentle; one fellow-star commented, 'Surely no one but a mother could have loved Bette Davis at the height of her career.' One of her bitchier witticisms (or do I mean wittier bitchicisms?) at that time bears repeating: she described a rival who had reputedly slept her way to stardom as 'the original good time that was had by all.'

' *The world is full of people whose notion of a satisfactory future is, in fact, a return to the idealised past* ' **Robertson Davies,** Canadian writer, in *A Voice from the Attic,* 1960

23

Tennis trophy

IN 1900 the president of the US National Lawn Tennis Association wrote to his British opposite number, 'One of our players here has offered us a Cup, to be a sort of International Challenge Cup. I enclose the conditions in a rough form. I trust that we shall both take a deep interest in them for many years to come. It might do a great deal for the game here, and possibly even with you it might be a help.' The player mentioned was Dwight F Davis, and the competition for the Davis Cup has taken place almost every year since 1900, except during the two World Wars. Dwight Davis (1879-1945) was still up at Harvard when he donated the cup (a 13-inch high sterling silver bowl weighing 217 ounces), but he had already twice been runner-up in the US singles championship. He went on to distinction in other fields, becoming US secretary of war (1925-9) and governor-general of the Philippines (1929-32). Britain last won the Davis Cup in 1936, since when it has belonged to either the USA or Australia.

A fighter for women's education: Emily Davies (1830-1921)

ONE OF THE GREAT figures of the women's rights movement in the 19th century, Emily Davies was the daughter of a Church of England clergyman. She was educated at home, and when her brothers went up to Cambridge she resolved one day to open a college for women there. So she did, but not for many years. Until her father died in 1860, Emily was expected, as an unmarried daughter, to live at home. But from about 1858 she was active in the women's movement. In 1862 she formed a committee, with herself as secretary, to press for the admission of women to Cambridge University examinations. This right was soon granted.

The next move, Miss Davies thought, was to establish a proper residential college for women students. But the influence of her vicarage background was still strong. She was determined that her carefully-selected young ladies should be kept well away from male undergraduates, in conditions of the utmost respectability. So she rented a house at Hitchin, 30 miles from Cambridge, and here, in October 1869, her new college opened with its first batch of five students. Despite this desperate concern for propriety, the little group were denounced as 'infidel ladies' by a clergyman who met them on the train to Cambridge!

But despite physically separating her girls from the University, Emily Davies was adamant that their studies should be identical with those of men students. She was bitterly opposed to current attempts to organize separate educational schemes for women. She rightly saw this as a sort of academic apartheid, with 'separate' just a polite word for 'inferior': *her* goal was nothing less than full equality.

The college at Hitchin slowly grew, and by 1872 had 13 students. That year three of the original girls passed their Tripos examinations. But it was becoming obvious that a 30-mile railway journey was a great hindrance to sharing the academic advantages of Cambridge, and Miss Davies reluctantly agreed to a move. To keep the girls safe from any distracting and improper contact with men, the site chosen was 'near but not in' the town — about two miles from the centre, in fact, near the village of Girton. A tutor and 15 students took up residence in 1873. Girton's formidable academic reputation was established from the start: Emily Davies had no use for fripperies and luxuries, and life at the college was austere and dedicated. (Things were very different at the other women's college started that this time, Newnham, where the principle of separate women's examinations made for a freer, more easy-going regime.) For the rest of her long life she continued to take a keen interest in Girton College, and she lived to see the number of students rise to nearly 200. Not until 1948, however, did Cambridge admit women as full members of the university on equal terms with men — thus achieving the aim of which Emily Davies had first dreamed almost exactly one hundred years before.

All-round entertainer

SAMMY DAVIS JUNIOR was born in Harlem in 1925. Living in an all-coloured community he encountered little racial prejudice until he entered the army during the war. When he did, he met it with his fists, and claims, 'I had scabs on my knuckles for the first three months in the army.' Soon, however, he discovered his talents as an entertainer, and from then on met hostility by just trying harder, taking it as a challege to win over every single member of his audience. In his long show-business career he has excelled as an all-round entertainer, the sort of versatile performer who can get up alone on a stage and keep an audience happy for hours with a series of turns — dancing, comic patter, acting, mimicry, singing. Certainly he has been extraordinarily successful: some time ago his income was said to be between two and three million dollars a year.

Davis never lost his awareness of racial prejudice; but he is free from bitterness and well able to joke about it. 'Being a star', he writes in his autobiography *Yes I Can*, 'has made it possible for me to get insulted in places where the average Negro could never hope to get insulted.' A big turning point in his life came in 1954, when he lost his right eye in a car accident, and shortly afterwards announced his conversion to Judaism, feeling a strong affinity between Negroes and Jews as oppressed peoples. This too he can treat as a joke, 'I'm a coloured one-eyed Jew — do I need anything else?'

Young Irishman: Thomas Osborne Davis (1814-1845)

THOMAS DAVIS, who died of scarlet fever in 1845 when only 30 years old, was one of the most influential leaders of the Irish people in the 19th century. Had he lived, the history of modern Ireland might have been very different. Yet all the most important events in his career were crammed into less than four years.

As a student at Trinity College, Dublin, Davis, who was a Protestant, made many Catholic friends. He read widely, especially in Irish history and literature, and became convinced of the need for national independence. Charming, sincere and immensely learned, he soon became very influential. In 1842, with two friends, he founded a newspaper, *The Nation*, which quickly became a great success. It set out to teach Irish people about their own country, and about what could be done to make it free. Rather to his own surprise, Davis found he had a talent for verse: one of the most popular features of the paper was the series of stirring patriotic ballads he wrote for it. Many of them were set to music and sung all over the country.

Davis's prose writing for *The Nation* was full of good sense. Every aspect of Ireland was touched on — from peat, whose enormous potential as a fuel he was one of the first to realize, to the Irish language, of which he wrote, 'To lose your native tongue, and learn that of an alien, is the worst badge of conquest — it is the chain on the soul. A

Creditor Davis . . . the lender

people without a language of its own is only half a nation.' Davis also planned a series of cheap paperback books about Ireland and Irish affairs: this, a very progressive idea for the time, was to be part of his grand scheme of educating ordinary Irish people in the traditions and culture of their country, as the best way of persuading them to work to make it a nation again.

The great Irish leader of this period, Daniel O'Connell, made Catholic emancipation his chief aim, and linked Irish nationalism with the Roman Catholic faith in a way which is still bringing sorrow and suffering to Ireland today. Davis set himself firmly against this, for he was convinced that Protestants and Catholics could be united in love of their country. O'Connell, moreover, was not a thorough-going nationalist: his aim was to repeal the 1800 Act of Union, and get Ireland back its own parliament under the Crown. Davis, on the other hand, believed in total freedom and was prepared if necessary to fight to achieve it. Those who agreed with him formed a group known as 'Young Ireland': they carried on his ideas after his death, and in 1848, when revolution was sweeping Europe, launched a rather incompetent and short-lived uprising. By this time Ireland had been broken by the horrors of the great potato famine of 1845-7, and 'Young Ireland' did not survive: but Thomas Davis is still remembered and honoured as one of the founders of the modern Irish nation.

Champion chinwagger

THE WOMEN'S WORLD RECORD for non-stop talking is held by Mrs Mary E Davis, who spoke for 110 hours 30 minutes on the radio in the USA. Most male chauvinists will be surprised to learn that the masculine record is nearly 40 hours longer!

Regency rake: Scrope Berdmore Davies (1782-1852)

ONE NIGHT IN 1808, a young gentleman called Scrope Berdmore Davies was drinking and dicing at a London gaming-house with some friends. At about four or five in the morning the friends, knowing when they had had enough, went home to bed: Davies, who was losing heavily, ignored their entreaties to come too, and went on gambling. Let one of his friends tell the rest of the story. 'Next day, being visited, about two of the clock, by some friends just risen with a severe headache and empty pockets, he was found in a sound sleep, without a night-cap, and not particularly encumbered with bed-clothes: a chamber-pot stood by his bed-side, *brim-full* of — *Bank Notes*! all won, God knows how, and crammed, Scrope knew not where; but *there* they were, all good legitimate notes, and to the amount of some thousand pounds.'

The friend who describes this incident is none other than Byron. Scrope Davies (whose first name, incidentally, rhymes with 'group' rather than 'grope') was one of the poet's closest friends, and a fairly typical rake and dandy of the kind we all associate with Regency England. His story, which goes on from scenes of riot and revelry to a lonely 32-year exile on the Continent, is worth telling for its own sake, quite apart from the links with Byron, but also because of the odd sequel, when Davies hit the headlines in a big way 124 years after his death.

Scrope Davies was the son of a country parson. He was sent to Eton, and picked up there the extravagant tastes and love of gambling which were to prove his ruin in the end. He then went on to Cambridge, becoming a Scholar and subsequently a Fellow of King's College. (No particular academic ability was required for this — a Scholar of Eton could more or less automatically end up a Fellow of King's.

He was then guaranteed an income, enough to live on though not in luxury, for the rest of his life, as long as he did not marry!)

Byron and Davies became friends in 1807. The young poet found Davies a delightful companion — carefree, witty, reckless, constantly entertaining. Byron had a depressive, sensitive streak in his character which all his life he tried to conceal (with considerable success) behind the public image of romantic amorality: Scrope Davies, in this respect, really was what Byron would have liked to be, enjoying wine and women and wild extravagance with unselfconscious gusto. With Davies and a couple of other like-minded friends, Byron began to sow his wild oats enthusiastically, attending rowdy, drunken parties in Cambridge and visiting London and Brighton (then the centre of fashionable society), where he gambled heavily and had a succession of affairs with ladies of easy virtue. Perhaps, though, the most notorious escapade the friends got up to together was the party Byron gave at Newstead Abbey, his ancestral home. The young men dressed up as monks, in habits hired from a theatrical costumier, and lived it up far into the night: there were drunken brawls, a maidservant fled screaming from the house, and a human skull filled with wine was passed round for toasts to be drunk.

For Byron all this was only a phase: fairly soon he was off on his first long tour on the Continent. Scrope Davies, on the other hand, lived this sort of life full-time. For many years he was that unusual thing, a professional gambler who actually made a profit. The incident with which I began was by no means his biggest win — one night in 1814 he won more than £6,000. It is not really possible to calculate what such a sum represents in modern money: a quarter of a million might be a reasonable guess. (For comparison, a farm labourer in 1814 earned about £35 a *year*.) But Davies knew how to be generous: on one occasion, having won a young man's entire fortune, he gave it back in return for a promise that he would never gamble again.

Davies's own luck changed in the end. After 1815 he began to drift deeper and deeper into debt. For a while he survived, borrowing from Peter to pay Paul, juggling money between his accounts with a number of banks, and still enjoying an occasional run of luck at the tables. But it could not last. In January 1820, with ruin and the debtor's prison hard on his heels, Davies escaped to the Continent and there, in Belgium or France, he stayed until his death, living fairly contentedly on the small income which still arrived regularly from King's College, and enjoying the company of the many Englishmen who visited him in the course of their travels.

So, a slightly pathetic, increasingly outdated figure, Scrope Davies passed to his almost unnoticed death. But it was not the end of his story. In 1976 a battered leather trunk in the vaults of Barclay's Bank, Pall Mall, was opened. It turned out to contain a mass of papers which Davies had crammed into it and deposited with his bankers 156 years before, when he was on the point of flying the country. The contents included many letters from Byron, two unknown poems by Shelley, an invitation from the Duke of Wellington, and numerous letters, bills, sketches and other documents — a 'time-capsule' of enormous interest which made the almost forgotten figure of Scrope Davies an even greater celebrity than he had been at the height of his wild and eventful career.

Soloist

DON DAVIS of Hollywood describes himself as 'the World's Smallest Full Orchestra.' Put another way, he is certainly the world's greatest one-man band, able to play four melody and two percussion instruments simultaneously without the help of electronics. Among the instruments he makes use of are an 'eight-prong pendular perpendicular piano pounder' and a 'semicircular chromatic radially-operated centrifugally sliding left-handed glockenspiel'!

President of the South:
Jefferson Davis (1808-1889)

JEFFERSON DAVIS, who led the Confederacy, the South, in the American Civil War, was born in Kentucky not 100 miles from the place where his great opponent, Abraham Lincoln, was born about a year later. (In personal appearance the two men were strikingly alike, which caused many quite unfounded rumours during the Civil War that they were related.) Davis was brought up in Mississippi where, after a brief spell in the army, he became a planter. For ten years he worked hard running his estate: he became deeply attached to his land, and to the southern way of life it represented. He owned slaves, but treated them kindly and paternally, and often shared their work in the fields.

In the Mexican War of 1846-8 Davis went back into the

' No civilised person ever goes to bed the same day he gets up ' **Richard Harding Davis**.

The Reverend D D Davis . . . the poor curate

army. He and his Mississippi Rifles made a brave stand at the battle of Buena Vista, and Davis found himself a popular hero. It was probably the worst thing that ever happened to him: the praise went to his head, and ever after he thought of himself as a born soldier with the makings of a great general. This attitude did not help him when he was in command of a nation at war and had authority over several generals who really were great.

From 1847 on Davis was active in politics, mainly as Senator for Mississippi. Over the next 14 years his opinion, like that of most Southerners, was moving towards a belief in some form of separation for the South. He was not in favour of out-and-out independence, however; he would have been quite happy with Southern self-government within the United States. What he did feel was essential, however, was that the South should have an open frontier, with the possibility of new states in the empty lands of the West opting for a Southern rather than Northern way of life. It was on this point that his final breach with Lincoln came, for Lincoln declared that though he would concede anything else, there must be no more slave states. On January 21 1861 Davis reluctantly announced to the Senate Mississippi's secession from the Union.

He did not particularly want to be president of the Confederacy: he would have much preferred to command the armed forces. But the general convention of Southern states chose him as a compromise — he was nobody's first choice, but everyone's second. The job was enough to daunt anyone. Davis had simultaneously to build a new nation and fight a war. The South had a white population a quarter that of the North; it had no heavy industries, no arms factories, and few mineral resources; its only assets were courage, confidence and cotton. All things considered, the confederacy did well to keep fighting for four years; and much of the credit must go to Jefferson Davis's powers of leadership.

Adversity brought out the best in Davis. Throughout the war he had to contend with a squabbling Congress, an obstructive vice-president, governors jealous for their states' rights, and virulent newspaper criticism which his democratic principles prevented him from censoring. Despite military defeats, lack of manpower and armaments, runaway inflation and his own desperately poor health, he remained resolute. But he was increasingly forced by the pressures of the war to abandon his own principles: up till now he had been a staunch defender of state rights, but his policies became increasingly centralist over questions like conscription and the compulsory purchase of supplies by the government.

By the winter of 1864-5 the Confederacy was crumbling. Davis, however, would not admit defeat. He even contacted the British government with an offer to emancipate the slaves in return for Britain's support in the war. (The suggestion, he was told, had come too late.) It is rather hard to follow Davis's thought processes at this point: if he was prepared to abandon slavery, just what was he fighting for? With that conceded, Lincoln would undoubtedly have offered generous terms. Davis, it seems, had come to believe that the war was being fought for Southern independence at any price — almost the opposite of his position four years earlier. His former confidence had hardened into total delusion: with the Confederacy falling apart, the troops deserting, the currency worthless, and Union troops marching, almost unopposed through the South, he could still speak of victory. It reminds one uncomfortably of the conduct in defeat of Napoleon or Hitler.

Reality finally broke through. The last Confederate

army surrendered on April 26, 1865, and on May 10, Davis was captured by Union troops. He spent two years in prison while his captors debated whether to put him on trial. In the end, probably fearing that a court of law might have justified him by deciding states had a right under the original constitution to leave the union, they set him free. He lived on for more than 20 years in comparative poverty. Many of his old friends in the North remained loyal to him during the war and after. He was, indeed, a man of great charm, courteous, dignified and warm-hearted: everyone admired his honesty and determination. But he was too inflexible to succeed as a politician; he could be overbearing and obstinate when his opinions were opposed. By nature he was a benevolent aristocrat — not a bad representative of the best members of the class of Southern gentlemen whose way of life he struggled to preserve.

Triple gold

THE WELSH LONGJUMPER Lynn Davis was three times voted British Athlete of the Year, in 1964, 1966 and 1967. In 1966 he became the first man ever to win gold medals at the Olympic, Commonwealth and European Games in a single year. (He was also, incidentally, the first Welsh athlete ever to win an Olympic gold medal.) Between 1963 and 1967 he had 17 successive wins at his event, a British record.

Joe Davis

POSSIBLY THE GREATEST BILLIARDS and snooker player of all time was the Englishman Joe Davis (1901-78). He won the world billiards title four times, in 1928-30 and 1932, and the world snooker title a record 15 times, in

1927-40 and 1946. He is also one of the few people ever to have officially achieved the world record break at snooker of 147 (often, though strictly speaking incorrectly, described as the highest possible break).

Joe's brother Fred carried on the family tradition by winning the world snooker championship eight times in nine years (1948 to 1956 — he missed it only in 1950). And more recently, in 1977, Steve Davis made a break of 147 at the age of 19, and turned professional the next year after a string of victories. He could stay at the top well into the next century — Joe Davis was at his peak in his fifties — so it looks as if Davis may continue to be a big name in snooker for many years to come.

Man of the theatre: Ivor Novello Davies (1893-1951)

One of the most versatile and successful men of the English theatre in this century was Ivor Novello, whose real name was Ivor Novello Davies. His mother, Clara Novello Davies, was a gifted conductor and music teacher, and Ivor quickly showed his own musical talent. He began to write songs in his teens, but his first big success came in 1914 with 'Keep the Home Fires Burning', one of the most popular patriotic songs of the First World War and a favourite marching tune for the troops. It made him a fortune, and brought him instant fame. He spent most of the war as an Air Ministry clerk (after proving disastrously unsuitable as an airman), but continued to write songs for musical comedies, and his first full-length score.

After the war Novello began to develop several careers simultaneously. His dark, handsome face, winning smile and glamorous profile made him a natural for the films. His parents, who had opposed his going on the stage, finally gave way and he appeared in his first play in 1921. His second musical comedy appeared the same year. Then in 1924 he achieved his ambition of becoming an actor-manager, by writing *The Rat* (in collaboration with Constance Collier), staging it himself at the Prince of Wales Theatre, and playing the lead. By now Novello was a celebrity, with crowds of fans besieging the stage door every night.

The rest of Ivor Novello's career was hardly more than a catalogue of successes. He composed 60 or so songs; starred in 17 films; and wrote more than 20 stage plays and musical comedies, in most of which he appeared himself. Among his greatest triumphs were the four musical plays he provided for the Theatre Royal, Drury Lane, which rescued that famous old playhouse from a bad patch. The most famous of these, *The Dancing Years*, was probably London's most popular show of the Second World War. Perhaps Novello's best work of all was *King's Rhapsody*, which appeared in 1949 and was still running in 1951 when he died suddenly of a heart attack.

All who knew him agree that Ivor Novello was not spoiled by success. He was a modest, affectionate person, and his immense talent was backed up by a willingness to take infinite time and trouble perfecting his work. Above all, perhaps, he was a happy man; and the very titles of his musical plays — *Careless Rapture, Glamorous Night, Perchance to Dream* and the rest — evoke the light-hearted, romantic view of life which he was able to share with millions of people.

A lifetime down the pit

DAVID DAVIES of Pontrhyfen, South Wales, worked underground as a coal miner for 73 years, from 1849 to

1922. He started work at the age of seven.

A woman in the army

MANY FOLK-SONGS TELL of girls enlisting as soldiers to
follow a husband or sweetheart to war. They are not all
pure fiction, as the story of Christian Davies proves. This
young Irishwoman inherited an inn in Dublin from her
aunt, and married a waiter there called Richard Welsh.
When he was forced to enlist as a soldier and sent to
Flanders, Christian set out to search for him. Calling herself
Christopher Welsh, she enlisted herself, and served in the
ranks from 1693 to 1697, suffering a wound and a spell as a
prisoner of war without her secret being discovered.

Four years of peace followed, and Christian went back
to Dublin; but when war broke out again, she went off to
Holland and re-enlisted. She fought as a dragoon under
Marlborough, and shortly after the battle of Blenheim met
her husband again after more than 12 years. Evidently she
actually *enjoyed* a soldier's life, for she persuaded Mr Welsh
to say she was his brother! At last, in 1706, her skull was
fractured by a shell at the battle of Ramillies, and the
surgeons found that she was a woman. She was naturally
dismissed from the ranks, but continued to live in camp as
a woman with her husband. He was killed in 1709, and her
second husband, a grenadier called Jones, in 1710. Two
years later she finally tired of camp life and came to
England. She was presented to Queen Anne, who
awarded her a pension of a shilling a day for life, and
married yet another soldier, called Davies — hence the
surname by which she is always known. She is buried,
appropriately enough, among the pensioners at Chelsea
Hospital.

'Dr' Davis . . . the quack

Miles Davis

ONE OF THE BIGGEST NAMES in modern jazz history is Miles Davis, trumpeter. During the 1940s he played with Charlie Parker, among others, and contributed to the development of the type of jazz known as 'Bebop'. Later he evolved a more personal style with his own small groups. His record *Kind of Blue* is reckoned to be one of the finest and most influential of all jazz recordings. In recent years he has more or less abandoned serious jazz for rock and pop.

Introducing Boswell to Johnson

TOM DAVIES (1712-1785) was an actor and bookseller in London. His bookshop has an honoured place in English literary history, for it was here that James Boswell first met Dr Johnson. Davies was an old friend of Johnson's, and Boswell, newly arrived from Scotland, made the bookseller's acquaintance and told him how anxious he was to meet Johnson. 'At last, on Monday the 16th of May, when I was sitting in Mr Davies's back parlour, after having drunk tea with him and Mrs Davies, Johnson unexpectedly came into the shop.' Davies at once introduced them. 'Recollecting his prejudice against the Scotch', writes Boswell, 'I said to Davies, "Don't tell where I come from." — "From Scotland", cried Davies roguishly. "Mr Johnson", said I, "I do indeed come from Scotland, but I cannot help it." "That, Sir," he retorted, "I find, is what a very great many of your countrymen cannot help".' Luckily, it would have taken more than this inauspicious beginning to put Boswell down: and by the end of the evening, when Davies was showing Boswell to the door, 'he kindly took upon him to console me by saying, "Don't be uneasy. I can see he likes you very well".' Davies was right; and from this meeting in his shop arose the friendship which was to result in the greatest of English biographies.

Bequest to a drunkard

WHAT, I WONDER, is the story behind this peevish sentence, found in the 1788 will of one David Davis of Clapham? *To Mary David, daughter of Peter Delaport, the sum of five shillings, which is sufficient to enable her to get drunk for the last time at my expense.*

The golden farmer

WILLIAM DAVIS was a prosperous farmer in 17th century Gloucestershire. He was happily married, with 18 children; a charming man, liked and respected by his neighbours, and known as 'the Golden Farmer' because he made all his payments in gold coin. Not until he was 63 years old did Davis's true story come out. For more than 40 years he had been a successful highwayman, the leader of a large gang. He worked in disguise, and used his local knowledge to select likely victims, such as farmers returning from cattle fairs or travelling to pay their rents. But he also went further afield for bigger game: on one occasion, single-handed, he robbed the Duchess of Albemarle on Salisbury Plain, despite her guard of four servants, taking three diamond rings and a gold watch. Before he was caught he had given up robbery for a few years, but went back on the road to raise money for some land he hoped to buy adjoining his farm. He was out of practice, and was recognised. He was hanged in London, and afterwards his body hung in chains from a gibbet on a common (the usual practice with condemned highwaymen) as a warning to others.

Steam engineer

AN AMERICAN INVENTOR, Phineas Davis, helped to design the first ever iron-clad steamboat, the *Codorus,* which had its trial run on the Susquehanna River, Pennsylvania, in November 1825. The idea did not catch on for some years. Meanwhile, Davis went on to design locomotives for the Baltimore and Ohio Railroad Company: but in 1835 he was killed when an engine he was testing was thrown off the track by a misplaced rail.

Queen of the musical glasses

THE WORD 'HARMONICA' nowadays usually refers to a mouth organ, but in the 18th century it was applied to a set of musical glasses. Benjamin Franklin, a man of many talents, was the inventor of a much-improved form of this instrument (he preferred to call it an 'armonica'), in which a row of glass bowls of different sizes rotates, half submerged in a trough of water. By touching the rims of the bowls with one's fingers it was possible to play tunes. (Anyone who has ever rubbed a wet finger round the rim of a wine glass will have a rough idea of how the instrument worked and what it sounded like.) A girl called Marianne Davies became famous for her skill on the harmonica. She was the talk of the town in 1762 and 1763, and even performed before some visiting Cherokee chiefs. She then went on tour on the Continent, to Paris, Vienna and Italy. Mozart was one of those who heard her perform. But there was something unpleasant about the continual contact of one's fingers with the revolving glass rims, and the sound, though piercingly sweet, was best heard in small doses. Miss Davies stuck it for ten years or so before retiring: it is said that 'her nerves were shattered by playing so much on an instrument of so peculiar a nature.'

Nell Gwynn's rival

MARY DAVIS was a talented actress and dancer in the 1660s. In one play she took the part of a shepherdess mad for love, and her rendering of a song 'My Lodging is on the Cold Ground' so charmed King Charles II that 'not long after it raised her from her bed on the cold ground to a bed royal.' Charles was generous to her, as to all his mistresses, setting her up with a fine house, a coach, and a ring worth £600. Nell Gwynn, Mary's rival as actress and royal mistress, was fond of practical jokes. One evening, hearing that Mary was to spend the night with the king, Nell asked her to supper beforehand, and gave her sweetmeats with a drug called jalap, a powerful laxative, mixed in. According to one version, the effects were so unfortunate that Charles forthwith dismissed Mary (though he did give her a pension of £1,000 a year). She was the mother of one of his 14 illegitimate children, Lady Mary Tudor, who married the Earl of Derwentwater. Some of her descendants are still living today.

Skulls galore

JOSEPH BARNARD DAVIS (1801-1881) was a country doctor whose hobby was craniology — the study of skulls. All his spare time and money was devoted to building up his collection of human skulls of all races and periods, each with careful notes on its measurements and history. In the end he had more skulls than all the museums in Britain put together. He published several books and papers on his pet subject, and just before he died sold his collection to the Royal College of Surgeons.

A surgeon's adventures

IN JANUARY 1598 a young barber-surgeon from London named William Davies set out in a merchant ship bound for the Mediterranean. It was 16 years before he saw England again, and when he did get home he sat down and wrote a lively account of his adventures. They included nearly nine years as a slave at the oar of a Florentine galley, a voyage to the Amazon as a ship's doctor, and a fight with pirates off the coast of Italy. In this fight another Englishman was killed, and Davies, not wanting the body to have a Roman Catholic funeral, proceeded to bury it himself. He was caught in the act by agents of the Inquisition, spent 16 days in an underground unlighted dungeon living on bread and water, and was finally helped to escape by an English shipowner. Nothing is known of his life after his book was published: but he had certainly earned a peaceful old age.

An English prima donna

CECILIA DAVIES, one of the best-known singers of the 18th century, spent much of her working career in Italy, where she was known as *L'Inglesina*, 'the English girl'. She was the first Englishwoman to be accepted by the Italians as a prima donna. Her proud boast was that she had taught singing to three queens, of France, Spain and Naples. Her later years were spent in poverty, and when she died in 1836 only an old nurse and a faithful servant attended her funeral.

Prince of bookies

ONE OF THE MOST FAMOUS bookmakers in the history of horse-racing was William Edmund Davies (1819-1879), known as the Leviathan (perhaps because of the vast scale of his business). He was a carpenter who began his career as a bookie by taking half-crown bets from his workmates, but by 1846 he had reached the top of his profession. He had a reputation unusual among bookmakers for honesty and prompt settling of his accounts. Some of his losses were enormous: after the 1852 Derby he had to pay out more than £100,000. But by 1957 he felt able to stop work, and spent the rest of his life in comfortable retirement in Brighton.

Self-sacrifice

SAMUEL DAVIS, 21 years old, was captured by Union forces during the American Civil War. He was spying for the South, and carrying amazingly accurate maps and information about the whereabouts and numbers of Northern troops. He was also carrying papers signed by 'Captain E Coleman', an alias used by another Southern spy, Henry Shaw. Shaw happened to be in the same jail as Davis, but none of his captors knew that he and the notorious 'Coleman' were one and the same. Davis was told that if he revealed the identity of 'Coleman' his life would be spared, but, knowing that to do so would be to sign Shaw's death warrant, he refused to speak. So he was hanged as a spy, while Shaw watched from the window of his cell.

Snoop Davies . . . the common informer